Discipleship Books:

The Holy Spirit

By

Philip Watson

Book 3

of the Trinity Series

Discipleship Books Ministry P Box 21731 Henderson, Auckland, New Zealand.

ISBN 978-0-473-30768-4

Dedication

Dedicated to my loving wife Dianne, and my three children, Andrew, Jonathon and Ruth.

My grateful thanks for allowing me to spend so much of my spare time writing these words.

Acknowledgments

My grateful thanks to Warren Portsmouth who patiently helped me review the manuscripts of my books. Warren suggested improvements and asked questions at appropriate points.

I also want to acknowledge the help of the Holy Spirit for inspiring me to write these books and for frequently reminding me of scriptures, relevant to topics, in each book.

Discipleship Books by Philip Watson

The Jesus Series:

Jesus The Ministry

Jesus The Incarnation

Jesus Changed Our Lives

The Trinity Series

The Father

The Son

The Holy Spirit

Other Books

The Cross and The Triangle

Successful Relationships

101 Spiritual Principles

1000 Great Quotes

Great Summaries

Contents

Introduction..1
Who is the Holy Spirit?...............................7
    The Father, The Son and Holy Spirit
    are:...8
        Eternal...8
        Creators..8
        Have great power............................8
        Have feelings..................................8
        Holy...9
        Loving..9
        Sources of Peace.............................9
        Counselors.......................................9
        Truth...9
  The Holy Spirit in the Bible.....................10
    In the Old Testament..........................10
    The Holy Spirit in the ministry of Jesus
   12
    In the New Testament Church............16
    Teaching about the Holy Spirit in the. 17
    Epistles..17
The Names and Titles of the Holy Spirit.............19
    Spirit of truth. John 14:17 23
    The 'holy' Holy Spirit..........................26
    The Advocate....................................26
Symbols of the Holy Spirit.............................29
    Fire...33
    Oil..34
    Dove...34
    Seal..36
    Water..37
    Wind...39

Symbols of the Holy Spirit and
functions of the Holy Spirit................42
    Fire...42
    Water...42
    Dove..42
    Oil...43
    Wind..43
    Seal..43
Roles of the Holy Spirit.........................45
  Role no 1: Communicator.............................46
  Role no 2: Creator.................................49
  Role no 3: Bearer of fruit..........................51
    How does the fruit grow? 53
  Role 4: Evangelist.................................54
  Role 5: The teacher................................56
  Role 6: The Reminder/Recaller......................58
  Role 7: Foreteller of the future.....................63
  Role 8: Convicts us of Sin and righteousness –
  John 16:8..67
The Divine Person..............................71
    The Spirit has a mind 73
    The Holy Spirit has emotions.............73
    The mind of the Spirit...................74
    Using our imagination:...................74
    The personality of the Spirit...............78
    Fellowship with the Holy Spirit...........81
Led By The Spirit...............................85
    How To Be Led By the Spirit of God. .89
    Learning to be led by the Spirit..........93
    Being led by the wrong party.............99
The Gifts of The Spirit.........................101
  Characteristics of the Holy Spirit, common to
  both Testaments...............................102
    Unique to one Testament.................103
    Gifts listed 1 Cor 12. 8-10................104
Our Attitude to the Holy Spirit..............107

Valuing the Holy Spirit 107
The Power of the Holy Spirit............110
Summary..119
Desiring the Holy Spirit....................119
Holy Spirit - The creator...................120
Holy Spirit - The Educator...............121
Holy Spirit - Who convicts, but does not condemn...121
Holy Spirit - The Evangelist..............121
Holy Spirit - Personal.......................121
Holy Spirit – works with, other members of trinity.............................121
Holy Spirit - Guide............................122
Holy Spirit and Church.....................122
World wide role.................................122
About Philip Watson...125

Introduction

Who is the Holy Spirit?

There is no equivalent to the Holy Spirit in any other religion. He has no specific location, no known physical features except that he was once seen in the form of a dove and another time, as tongues of fire. He has no known beginning and a name that only tells us he is 'holy', and 'spirit'. In the King James version of the Bible He is called "The Holy Ghost" and in many ways, that seems the most appropriate title.

The Holy Spirit is mentioned in the first and last chapters of the Bible, and often in between. I suggest that, though the Holy Spirit 'appears' to have played the role of 'silent partner' in the Bible, he has played a far greater role in the events of the Bible and the Church, than most give him credit for.

When I first became a Christian, I was confused about who the Holy Spirit was and his relevance to the Christian life. I could understand God being the creator and Jesus being our savior, so why was there a need for a Holy Spirit?

As a new Christian I noted that Jesus said the Holy Spirit would come on the disciples in "power". Those words conveyed the idea that the Holy Spirit was some kind of power, something like a divine, electrical current. But then there were Paul's words about being " filled with the Spirit." So was the Holy Spirit some sort of divine vapor, who filled people?

Then there were other references in the Bible to the Holy Spirit that only seemed to confuse the picture. Jesus called the Holy Spirit the "Spirit of truth", "counselor"' and "teacher".

As a new Christian I thought, 'It does not matter that I cannot connect these various images of the Holy Spirit together. I am sure that one day I will. If I just listen to enough sermons and read enough books, it will just be a matter of time!'

Since setting out to understand the Holy Spirit many years ago, I have come to another, surprising conclusion. I/we, will never fully understand the Holy Spirit this side of heaven. The reason is this. We are mortal beings, trying to understand the eternal, and we will never fully understand beings who live in every dimension of time and space.

If that is the bad news, we will never fully understand the Holy Spirit, this side of heaven. The good news is

1. I believe we are given in Scripture, all we need to know about the Holy Spirit.

2. The Holy Spirit is more than willing to help any person who wants to understand him more. He is after all called, "the teacher" and "the counselor".

3. Though our knowledge of the Holy Spirit may never be complete, this side of heaven, setting out on the journey to understand the Holy Spirit, is a journey well worth undertaking.

Forty years after committing my life to Jesus Christ, I have made a lot of progress in understanding who the Holy Spirit is. During that time, there have been two significant, 'leaps' forward in my knowledge. Those leaps are expanded in chapters 3 and 4.

One leap in knowledge came through studying the various names of the Holy Spirit. Through this study, I gained a much greater understanding of who the Holy Spirit is.

The second major leap forward occurred when I realized the Holy Spirit was 'a divine person' - in the same way that the risen Jesus and God the Father are, divine persons.

But progress has not only been in the quantity of knowledge. Progress has also been in the quality of knowledge. I have come to appreciate the *marvelous* nature of the Holy Spirit.

It is my hope and prayer that by reading this book, you will begin to hold the Holy Spirit in high esteem, and that words such as amazing, marvelous, and awesome, will seem appropriate words to describe the Holy Spirit.

Jesus hinted at the marvelous nature of the Holy Spirit when he said. "It is for your good that I am going away. Unless I go away, the Counselor will not come to you".... John 16:7

Jesus was saying, I am going but something even *better* will replace me. I am sure the first disciples did not share Jesus' enthusiasm about his departure, and they could not understand how the coming of the Holy Spirit would be to their benefit, or to their advantage.

That statement of Jesus, tells us three things about the Holy Spirit.

> 1. The time after Jesus' ascension to heaven is to be the 'era of the Holy Spirit' in the Church. These words of Jesus remind us that they worked in tandem to create the Church. Jesus came, to lay the foundation of the Church, but after his ascension, the Holy Spirit has come to grow the Church, on the foundation Jesus laid.

> 2. The Holy Spirit will come for the 'benefit' of both individuals, and the Church corporately.

A final word in this Introduction, to this book. In all three books in this series about the members of the trinity, I have made a point of supporting what is written with Scriptural references. That basis is probably even more important in this book about the Holy Spirit, because if Scripture is not the basis for our understanding of the Holy Spirit, the Holy Spirit can become the creation of your or my; personal opinion or speculation or tradition.

Further, if inspired Scripture is not the basis of this book, we may limit what the Holy Spirit can do based on our own limitations, rather than say "Wow, that is what the Holy Spirit can do!"

Before beginning to explore the different aspects of the Holy Spirit in the pages of this book, I invite the readers to pray this prayer.

> *"Welcome Holy Spirit! Please confirm those truths about you that I already know, and I ask you to highlight any aspects of your nature and abilities that I am not familiar with – for you are "teacher", "counselor" and the "Spirit of truth". Amen"*

Chapter 1

Who is the Holy Spirit?

This question leads on from the introduction.

The short answer to the question, "Who is the Holy Spirit?", is that the Holy Spirit is both 'of' God and 'from' God. We believe the Holy Spirit comes from God or was created 'by' God. This belief is based on Paul's letter to the Church at Rome. He wrote

> "For from him (God) and through him are all things." Rom 11:36

Although the noun 'things' is impersonal and the Holy Spirit is personal; we can assume that the Holy Spirit was made by God along with all the other heavenly beings, because the word 'all', is inclusive. Paul also wrote

"We have not received the spirit of this world but the Spirit who is **from God**."

Many verses in the Bible make it clear that the Holy Spirit is of the same nature as God. We can see that the Holy Spirit has the same nature and comes from God, when we compare the characteristics they share.

The Father, The Son and Holy Spirit are:
Eternal

Gen 21:33

Heb 9:14

John 1:1

Creators

Gen 1:1

Gen 1:1

John 1:3

Have great power

Jude 25

Zech 4:6

Rev 19:16

Have feelings

Exod 3:7

Eph 4:30

John 11:35

Holy

Rev 4:8

John 14:26

John 4:34

Loving

Deut 7:7

Rom 15:30

John 11:5

Sources of Peace

Phil 4:7

Gal 5:22

John 14:27

Counselors

Rom 11:34

John 14:16

Isa 9:6

Truth

Psa 31:5

John 14:17

John 14:6

The above list is not exhaustive, but readers

will be to see that the Holy Spirit shares the same nature and qualities as, the Father and Son. We should expect any being created by God and living in constant fellowship with God (like the Holy Spirit does see 1 Cor 2:10), to have the same qualities as God, the Father.

The Holy Spirit in the Bible

A clearer understanding of who the Holy Spirit is, is obtained by reviewing references to the Holy Spirit in the pages of the Bible.

In the Old Testament

The first Old Testament reference to the Holy Spirit is found in Genesis chapter one.

> "...and the Spirit of God was hovering over the waters." Gen 1.2

The Holy Spirit is frequently mentioned in the Old Testament, but usually briefly. Sometimes the references are so brief, that it is easy to miss them. However, the Holy Spirit was involved with the people in the Old Testament, in the same way he was involved in Jesus' ministry, and in the New Testament Church.

The most frequently used phrase to describe the Holy Spirit is "The Spirit of the Lord came upon...." When the Holy Spirit came upon various people in the Old Testament, some prophesied, some became bold, some performed miracles.

The Holy Spirit equipped leaders in the Old Testament, just as he did in the New Testament. Virtually every leader or prophet the Old Testament was connected to the Holy Spirit. Examples include:

- "God spoke to Moses.. and I will take the Spirit that is on you and put the Spirit on them. (the elders)" Num 11.17

- "The Spirit of the Lord came upon a group of seventy elders" Num 11.25

- "When the Holy Spirit came upon Gideon, he was suddenly bold enough to lead Israel to war with the people who were oppressing them." Judges 6:34

- "Samson's great strength came when the Spirit of the Lord was upon him." Judges 14:6

- "From the time that David was anointed by the prophet Samuel, the Spirit came upon him." 1 Sam 16:13

- The Holy Spirit stayed with David his whole life. King David, near the end of his life wrote. "The Spirit of the Lord spoke through me; his word was on my tongue." 2 Sam 23:2 After the Prophet Nathan had told David that God had seen his adultery and murder, David repented and pleaded with God. "Do not take your Holy Spirit from me." Psa 51:11

• When Elisha started his ministry, prophets standing nearby noted that Elisha had the same power to do miracles as Elijah. They exclaimed, "The Spirit of Elijah is resting on Elisha."....2 Kings 2:13-15

• Isaiah was sent by God with his Spirit. Isa 48:16

• Ezekiel wrote, "Then the Spirit of God came into me…" Ezek 3:24.

• Daniel's ability to interpret dreams came from the Spirit of God in him. Dan 4:8.

The Holy Spirit in the ministry of Jesus

Jesus declared at the beginning of his ministry, "The Spirit of the Lord is upon me"....Luke 4:18. After the seventy two disciples had returned from their missionary journey, Luke wrote that "Jesus was full of joy through the Holy Spirit,...." Luke 10:21

Jesus recognized that his disciples would

need the Holy spirit too if they were to be effective. So when he sent the first disciples out on their first missionary journey, he said. "Receive the Holy Spirit."

Later in his ministry, Jesus gave them specific details about, and impressed on them the need for the Holy Spirit. See John chapters 14-16. Before his ascension, Jesus said to his disciples "... in just a few days you will be baptized with the Holy Spirit." Acts 1:5 (NLT)

Jesus teaching about the Holy Spirit

Jesus made it clear to Nicodemus that unless someone is 'born again', they cannot see the kingdom. John 3:3. By the words "born again", Jesus was meaning "Everyone can be and needs to be "born of the Spirit", to enter the kingdom of heaven. John 3:5

Another time, Jesus raised the same issue he had raised with Nicodemus. He said,

"The Spirit gives life;" John 6:63.

What Jesus was meaning is only the Holy Spirit gives us spiritual life. Paraphrased,

'With the Holy Spirit there is spiritual life.' 'Without the Holy Spirit, there is no spiritual life.'

Credit must be given as it is implied that Nicodemus took Jesus' words on board and he was one of the many teachers of the law, who became disciples of Jesus.

The most significant teachings Jesus gave about the Holy Spirit, are found in John chapters 14 -16. These chapters of John could be compared to a check list a person writes for themselves before departing on a long journey.

Most people contemplating such a journey ask a number of questions. "Have I got this and that in my bag?", "Is my passport up to date?". "Do I have my medications?" etc.

John chapters 14 to 16, were like a check list of vital information for the disciples, before Jesus departed this Earth. By teaching the disciples about the Holy Spirit, Jesus was preparing the disciples for the journey they would begin, once He had returned to heaven.

Jesus knew, they would have to rely on the Holy Spirit to help them once he was gone.

New aspects of the nature of the Holy Spirit were revealed, in this pre-crucifixion talk. Bible scholars talk of 'progressive revelation' and Jesus took their knowledge of the Holy Spirit to a new level at this time.

The Samaritan woman who met Jesus at Jacob's well spoke of the type of progression in knowledge that the Messiah was expected to bring. She said

> "I know that the Messiah"...is coming. When he comes, he will explain everything to us." John 4:25

And that is what the disciples received at that time. Jesus began to use a different name for the Holy Spirit. The disciples would have been familiar with the term "the Spirit of the Lord" from their knowledge of the Old Testament. During this pre-crucifixion talk, Jesus added the prefix "holy" to the Spirit of God, so that we now call him, "the Holy Spirit."

Holiness had always been part of the nature of the Spirit, but it was not until Jesus began to add 'Holy' to his name, that the Church came to understand that holiness was an integral part of the nature of the Holy Spirit.

Jesus also began to use the personal pronoun "He", implying that the Holy Spirit was a divine person, or divine personal being. Jesus also indicated that they would know the Holy Spirit in a new dimension. He said

> "he lives with you and will be 'in' you". John 14:17.

He also said that the Holy Spirit would be a 'teacher' and a 'counselor' and remind the disciples of Jesus' teachings. Subsequent chapters will highlight the significance of these roles.

In the New Testament Church.
When the Holy Spirit came on the disciples during the feast of Pentecost, there was a boldness evident in them that was completely lacking during the 'Passover festival' in Jerusalem. During the Passover festival when Jesus was arrested, the disciples scattered like scared rabbits, and hid behind closed doors and Peter denied to a servant girl, that he was a disciple of Jesus.

However, after the Holy Spirit had come on them in power, those same disciples, were completely different people. They could not keep quiet about Jesus, and boldly* preached about him. The Holy Spirit also gave the disciples the ability to speak in the languages of the Jews assembled from all over the Roman Empire.

*That boldness, was also characteristic of people in the Old Testament, when the Holy Spirit came on them.

Teaching about the Holy Spirit in the Epistles

At the feast of Pentecost, the Holy Spirit came like the sound of wind and tongues of fire (external manifestations), but after Paul was converted, he began to write to the New Testament Churches about the work of the Spirit on the 'inside' of Christians.

These teachings about the work of the Holy Spirit 'in' each believer will be reviewed later in this book.

This chapter has been a brief summary of the nature, the work and the roles of the Holy Spirit. The Bible tells us that the Holy Spirit will continue to work actively with the Church, until Jesus comes again.

18   Who is the Holy Spirit?

Chapter 2

The Names and Titles of the Holy Spirit

There are many names and titles given to the Holy Spirit in the Bible, principally by Jesus. As I explain below, these titles were not given by Jesus, just to fill up the pages of the New Testament. These names or titles are 'exact' descriptions, of the nature of the Holy Spirit.

Jesus indicated to Nicodemus why he was able to be very specific about the names of the Holy Spirit. He said "... how then will you believe if I speak of heavenly things? No one has ever gone into heaven except the one who came from heaven - the Son of Man."

John 3:13

The information Jesus was able to give the first disciples about the Holy Spirit (and other subjects), was because he came directly from the throne-room of heaven. So when Jesus used names or titles for the Holy Spirit such as "Spirit of truth" or "teacher", "counselor" Jesus was using those titles because he knew the Holy Spirit intimately, and had come from heaven.

Jesus' intimate knowledge of the nature of the Holy Spirit became apparent when I was a young Christian. At that stage, I could recall reading in John's Gospel a variety of titles for the Holy Spirit like "comforter", "counselor" and "the Spirit of truth"; but they did not mean anything to me.

It was information that I assumed to be true because Jesus had spoken those words - but what did they mean? One experience, illustrated to me that these titles are exact descriptions of the nature of the Holy Spirit.

At that stage, I was part of a group of Christians who enjoyed one another's company and fellowship. As we met one evening, we were urged to be quiet and were told that one of the group's leaders, wanted to say something. In faltering words, he admitted to his fellow leaders and those he had led, that the reason for his rushed marriage, was that his fiancée was pregnant. Today, such an event would not raise any eye brows.

Because this admission came out of the blue, most of us were lost for words - particularly because the man had the courage to tell the truth to the people he had been leading face to face.

We may have heard about this pregnancy through the grape vine. In this case, the youth leader chose to confess his sins to the whole group, face to face. We fell silent, not knowing what to say.

I was by the window on that windless night and it may have been a coincidence, but I don't think so. The curtains to that room began to move gently, and as they did, the comforting presence of the Holy Spirit began to fill the room.

This was a new understanding of the Holy Spirit to me. It was very different from the way the Holy Spirit came at Pentecost, like the sound of a rushing wind. With this experience, the Holy Spirit came like a gentle breeze.

I later asked myself. 'Why did the Holy Spirit come into the room, and fill it with his comforting presence?' Then I recalled what Jesus had said about the Holy Spirit. He had called Him, "the Spirit of truth". So the Holy Spirit came because this man had the courage to tell the truth, face to face to those he led. Because he had spoken the truth, the Holy Spirit came into that room as "comforter". John 14:26

Suddenly, two titles Jesus used for the Holy Spirit had meaning. "Spirit of truth" and "comforter".

An explanation for readers whose versions of the Bible do not have the word "comforter" for the Holy Spirit. Older versions of the Bible use "comforter". Modern translations may use words like "Counselor" or "Advocate". If that sounds confusing, a word of explanation is necessary.

Sometimes translators have difficulty trying to find the best English word for modern day readers when the language they are translating from, was current 2000yrs ago. With the Greek language, translators have to choose between a number of 'possible' meanings and then a number of English words, that may be appropriate.

It is sometimes not a clear matter of right or wrong, but opting for one English word to represent the original Greek word. The Greek word *Parakletos* which different versions of the Bible render as "comforter" and "counselor" and "advocate", means

> *To comfort, encourage, exhort. Greek writers used the word for a legal adviser or advocate.*

So there is a sense in which, all of those choices are right. The difficulty for translators being, they have to choose a single word, when a number of words could be appropriate – including the word, "comforter".

Spirit of truth. John 14:17

That experience also highlighted what Jesus meant when he called the Holy Spirit, "the Spirit of truth". There are a number of ways in which the Holy Spirit reveals himself as "the Spirit of truth".

- **1** Jesus said that the Holy Spirit convicts people of guilt, in regard to sin, righteousness and judgment. John 16:8 When people respond to the Gospel message, they are responding first of all because the message has been proclaimed - but also because the Holy spirit has been working in the heart of that person, to convince them of the 'truth' that they have sinned.

- **2** The Holy Spirit focuses on truth is in

our personal lives. Ananias and Sapphira lied to the Church about how much money they received from selling land and had their dishonesty exposed. Peter said to Ananias, "how is it that Satan has filled your heart that you have lied to the Holy Spirit"...Acts 5:4 and later he said to Sapphira, "How could you agree to test the Spirit...Acts 5:9

The Holy Spirit acted that way as a warning, but I believe that being open to the Spirit, is not only about being led to do some great work for the Lord. The Holy Spirit (the Spirit of truth) is equally concerned about what we do and say, away from Church - during the other 6 days of the week.

The Holy Spirit does not condemn people like Satan does, but sometimes gently and patiently asks us to consider what we are involved in, or the way we are doing a particular activity. I think of a Christian who took money from his business partner's account without his knowledge. When asked to explain "why he had taken the money", he said something like this. "It is all part of business".

As far as the Holy Spirit is concerned, there is no such thing as separate compartments to our lives. One compartment called 'the

Church part' (i.e. what we do and say and how we appear in Church), and the 'business part'. That is what Ananias and Sapphira had tried to do. As far as the Holy Spirit is concerned; truth is important in every part of our life – 24/7

It is because of the graciousness of the Holy Spirit, we are usually not called to account for the 'gray' transactions we make. If, however, we were to tune in to what the Spirit is saying, he may gently put his finger on a few of the gray areas of our life, and ask us to consider the truth.

- **3** The first three chapters of the book of Revelation contain messages from Jesus, to the Apostle John, about the health of seven Churches in Asia. In that vision, Jesus spoke to John about activities in those churches that pleased him - and activities and attitudes that grieved Him.

    Though Jesus told John about the health of seven specific churches, he is concerned about the health of every church. Jesus will not necessarily speak in a vision to the leaders of every church. His advice to the leaders of every church is "Listen to what the Spirit is saying ..."

- **4 T**he 4th way the Holy Spirit focuses on

truth; is in our worship. Jesus said that the Father wants us to worship him, "in spirit and in truth". John 4:24. It is hard to know exactly what Jesus meant by these words; but there is a gem contained in these words; apart from the specific meaning. The gem is. The 'how, when, where or why' of worship does not matter. All that God is concerned about is; that we worship him from our heart; or in truth.

The 'holy' Holy Spirit.

We are so used to calling the Holy Spirit, the Holy Spirit, we overlook the fact that he is 'holy'! The Holy Spirit has always been holy!

Prior to Jesus time on Earth, the word 'holy', was only used once to describe the Spirit of God. i.e. In Psalm 51. The adjective 'holy', only became a normal part of the title of the Spirit of God after Jesus began adding the adjective 'Holy' the "Spirit of God's" name. The holiness of the spirit of God is reflected in what pleases him and grieves him. Eph 4:25-32

The Advocate

It has already been mentioned earlier in this chapter, that the Greek word 'Parakletos' translated by some versions as 'comforter', can equally legitimately be translated as 'advocate'. Paul wrote about this role as advocate in the book of Romans.

> *"...because the Spirit intercedes for the saints in accordance with Gods will." Rom 8.27*

That is who an advocate is. Someone who represents us. A representative who puts our case to God.

Chapter 3

Symbols of the Holy Spirit

This chapter is a continuation of the last chapter. There are six symbols of the Holy Spirit in the Bible and possibly a seventh - the seven lamps. Each of these symbols are additional windows to help us understand the Holy Spirit.

The six symbols are:

- fire

- water

- oil

- a dove

- a seal

- wind.

Before reviewing each of these symbols, and their meaning, I will digress a little to ask and answer the question. "Why did the Holy Spirit come on Jesus in the form of a dove at his baptism and later on the disciples, in the form of fire accompanied by the sound of rushing wind?"

The Holy Spirit could have come on Jesus at his baptism (without appearing as a dove) and Jesus would have known about it; and on the disciples at the feast of Pentecost without appearing as a tongue of fire, and the disciples would have known.

Surely that is what is important, the Holy Spirit descending on Jesus and falling on the disciples, not the outward appearance?

The way the Holy Spirit came upon Jesus as a dove at his baptism, and as tongues of fire at the feast of Pentecost is in fact consistent with what God had done elsewhere in the Bible.

Examples include:

- God appearing to Moses in a burning bush
- a pillar of cloud by day and a pillar of fire

> by night, when the Hebrew people were being led through the desert
- a bright star in the sky at Jesus birth
- a bright light on the road to Damascus, when Saul heard Jesus speaking.

I suggest the reason these visual signs occurred is because:

> *In any event important to salvation history, God in his wisdom decided that visual signs are necessary for the human beings involved, that heaven was taking these events, seriously. God wanted the humans involved to know, that He was doing something very special!*

When the Holy Spirit appeared as a dove at Jesus' baptism, God spoke from heaven in a voice the disciples could hear. Jesus said afterwards.

> "This voice is for *your benefit*, not mine"... John 12:30 (italics added).

So we can also assume that when the Holy Spirit came on the disciples at the feast of Pentecost like tongues of fire and with the sound of wind, it was for the 'benefit' of the disciples and the unbelievers in Jerusalem at that time.

Prior to the feast of Pentecost, Jesus had

promised the Holy Spirit would come on the 12 disciples. When the Holy Spirit came, it was in a form they could *see*. In a form they could *hear,* and one they could *feel*. The coming of the Spirit was *confirmed* by the fact that they received the ability to speak many languages from around the Roman Empire. Languages they had never learned.

The feast of Pentecost has been called the 'birthday of the Church', and the disciples would look back and say to themselves "We were in no doubt that day the Holy Spirit came" and "We were in no doubt this was time Jesus had told us to wait for", when he said

> "wait for the coming of the gift my Father promised" Acts 1:4.

And we can see that it was the beginning of the fulfillment of Jesus' words "You will be my witnesses in Jerusalem, Judea and Samaria, and to the ends of the earth" because in Jerusalem that day were Jews from all over the Roman Empire and the Holy Spirit gave the disciples the ability to speak the various languages of the Empire. Acts 1:8 (N.I.V)

To return to the question raised at the beginning of this chapter about symbols. God in his wisdom knows that sometimes we understand truth better when we have a symbol to represent that truth. The following symbols of the Holy Spirit, are just that, symbols. But if we view them through our spiritual eyes, we will understand the Holy Spirit better.

Fire

A fire in a log burner or a fire-place at home, is lit to bring warmth. A fire burning in a metal smelter is there to extract metal from the ore through a process of purifying and refining. When fire is mentioned in the Bible, it is often associated with purifying and refining. In the book of Isaiah, the prophet predicted that God would bring judgment on Jerusalem by a "spirit of judgment and a spirit of fire." Isa 4:4 (NIV)

Other Scriptures that associate fire with cleansing and refining, are found in the books of Malachi 3:2 and 1 Cor 3:13. No one likes refining, no one likes purifying, but the purpose of refining is to create pure metal, be it steel, gold or silver.

Fire is also a form of heat and energy that we can either fan or dampen. With the picture of a flame burning, we can understand the reference by the apostle Paul to the Holy Spirit.

> "Do not put out the Spirit's fire."
> 1Thess 5:19 (NIV)

For examples on how to fan the Spirit's flame, or dampen the Spirit's flame, please read 1 Cor 5:12-28

Oil

Oil is symbolic for anointing. Leaders like David were anointed with oil to consecrate them to God. When David was anointed with oil to become King, the Bible says, "and from that day on the Spirit of the Lord came on David in power." 1 Sam 16:13

At the beginning of his ministry, Jesus read this passage from the prophet Isaiah:

> "The Spirit of the Lord is on me, because he has **anointed** me...
> Luke 4:18 (boldness added).

Can you see the correlation between anointing and the Holy Spirit?

When someone is consecrated to God's service, the Holy Spirit anoints that person for service.

Dove

The dove represents purity, peace, gentleness and new life.

1. The Spirit is holy and also the spirit of truth. So the symbol of a pure dove, is a very apt symbol for the purity of the Holy Spirit.

2. A dove represents peace, and peace is a fruit of the Spirit.

3. The dove is also a gentle bird, and gentleness is also a fruit of the Spirit. When the Holy Spirit came on Jesus at his baptism; it is probable that the Holy Spirit descended on Jesus like a gentle dove. When the Holy Spirit wants our attention, it is not usually by force; rather it is a gentle prompting.

4. In the book of Genesis, after the rains ceased, but the Earth was still flooded, so Noah sent out a dove to see if it could find any life. Eventually the dove returned with a twig in it's beak, indicating that there was life. The dove returning with a twig (representing life) is symbolic of other ways the Holy Spirit, gives life. Jesus spoke of being, "born of the Spirit" - meaning new spiritual life. John 3:5

Seal

Paul wrote

> "Having believed, you were marked in him with a seal, the promised Holy Spirit, who is a deposit guaranteeing our inheritance until the redemption of those who are God's possession ..." Eph 1:13 (NIV)

Paul's words convey the importance of the Holy Spirit as a seal. Important people in most eras affix seals to their letters. These seals not only conveyed the importance of the person, but also their office. So the seal of the Emperor or regional Governor was affixed to a letter, and only those authorized could open it.

The Apostle Paul is conveying this same idea by calling the Holy Spirit a seal. It is as if, when God looks down from heaven on people in whom the Holy Spirit dwells, God sees the seal of the Holy Spirit, and recognizes that person as His son or His daughter.

> *We mortal people are marked with, immortality. We sinful people, have been marked with the seal of a Holy God.*

> —   Phillip Watson

A woman involved in fortune-telling, reading palms, tarot cards and auras etc, said. "I can always tell who the Christians are, because of the presence of the Holy Spirit in them." She went on to make a telling comment. "The difference between Christians and us, is that we know how much power and knowledge there is in the spiritual realm whereas usually, they do not."

There is a positive side to her statement. We have the Spirit of the 'living God', residing in our spirits, as a seal; a deposit - of what is to come. That seal is of far greater importance than the seal of any Emperor, President or Prime Minister. It is the seal of the eternal, living God.

Water

Jesus associated water and the Holy Spirit a number of times. He said to Nicodemus

> "... no one can enter the kingdom of God unless they are born of 'water and the Spirit'." John 3:5 (NIV)

Water purifies and cleanses, that is why water is the medium for baptism. Paul wrote

> "For we were all baptized by one Spirit into one body...." 1 Cor 12:13.

When a person is baptized in water they die to the old life and come out a new person - renewed and cleansed. Jesus also associated water and the Holy Spirit when he said,

> " you will be baptized with the Holy Spirit." Acts 1:5

There is another way Jesus associated water and the Holy Spirit. He spoke of rivers of living water flowing out of a person. John 7:38 In that context, the Holy Spirit is like life-giving water that flows from a spring, into parched lands. And we know from other biblical verses that we Christians are meant to be people who are, conduits of this life-giving water.

At the beginning of his ministry Jesus read the words of the prophet Isaiah, beginning with, "The Spirit of the Lord is on me to:

- preach good news

- proclaim freedom

- recovery of sight

- release of the oppressed

- proclaim the year of the Lord's favor Luke 4:18-19

Jesus came to be a conduit of the life-giving waters of the Holy Spirit resulting in freedom, healing, sight and the Lord's favor.

Wind

When Jesus was talking to Nicodemus, he explained that the Holy Spirit is like the wind.

> "The wind blows where ever it pleases. You hear its sound, but you cannot tell where it comes from or where it is going. So it is with everyone who is born of the Spirit."
> John 3: 8

This analogy to the wind tells us two important features about the Holy Spirit. The Holy Spirit blows where 'he' wills, not where 'we' will. And it is as if Jesus is saying: "I would like the Holy Spirit to be the wind in your sails."

Many times in history and in the Church today, people have tried to box the Holy Spirit into set roles and actions. The idea of the Holy Spirit blowing like the wind, prompting whom he wills, when he wills; goes against the natural human inclination, to be in control.

I thought about Jesus' analogy to the Holy Spirit being like the wind that blows where it wills, when I was standing by a rock which was about 50 yards high and about 100 yards around the base. There were other smaller rocks around this rock. The wind that was blowing at the time, had to blow around the sides of the rock. Naturally the wind could not go through the rock, so it blew around either side. I had no idea where the wind came from or where it was going, like the analogy of Jesus to the Holy Spirit in John 3:8

When someone resists the Holy Spirit, they are being like an immovable rock which forces the Holy Spirit to blow around and past them, or their organization. This grieves God the Father who said:

> "My Spirit will not always contend with man forever for he is mortal." Gen 6:3.

An unyielding rock, is not the type of person the Holy Spirit would like to encounter. Below, I have tried to portray the type of person, the Holy Spirit would like to encounter - based on Jesus parable of the soils.

There are flowers and wheat growing in a field. They grow because of the sun and rain provided by God the Father. They are rooted into the soil, which is Jesus Christ. The wind (the Holy Spirit) causes the stalks to bend, and they grow strong as a result of bending to the wind of the Holy Spirit. This enables them to bear more fruit.

The blowing of the wind of the Spirit through the field of wheat, allows pollens to spread and for the species to multiply. And because they have allowed the wind of the Spirit to blow through the field, the wheat provides food for others and the flowers - fragrance and beauty.

The second important truth we can draw from Jesus comparison of the Holy Spirit to the wind is the idea that he is blowing past, seeking a person to fill. Paul wrote.

> "Instead be filled with the Spirit."
> Eph 5:18

However, the Holy Spirit is not the only being in the spiritual world, who has that goal. When God asked Satan where he had been, Satan replied

> "From roaming through the earth and going back and forth in it." Job 1:7

See also Luke 11:24.

With two spiritual forces (the Holy Spirit and demons) looking for homes in men and women, we determine, which one it will be.

Symbols of the Holy Spirit and functions of the Holy Spirit

Often in the Bible there is a correlation between one truth and another. This is also true of the symbols of the Holy Spirit, for those symbols relate to the way the Holy Spirit, does work in our lives.

Symbol	Working of Holy Spirit
Fire	
cleanses	'Holy' Spirit works to keep us
refines	holy & pure, refines our nature. Cf fruit of Spirit.
Water	
Purity	Cleanses -assoc with baptism.
new life	New birth by Spirit. John 3:5
flows	From Christians into parched lives.
Dove	
Peace	Peace is a fruit of the Spirit. Gal 5:22
gentleness	Gentleness is a fruit of the Spirit.
Purity	The Spirit is holy and Spirit of truth.

new life	New life in creation and in our spirit.

Oil

Anoints Luke 4:18	Sanctifies for Gods purposes. - -

Wind

Fills	Filled with Spirit Eph 5:18
blows	Seeks people to lead. Rom 8:14

Seal

Ownership	Confirms adoption as children of God. Rom 8:16

Chapter 4

Roles of the Holy Spirit

Today it is a standard marketing ploy to market most mechanical or electrical products as 'multi purpose' or 'multi role' or 'multi-functional'. The car that will serve well for business, family and recreational purposes. The kitchen blender that will pulp, blend and juice most foods. The fitness equipment that will enable you to strengthen many parts of your body with just the one piece of equipment.

The current trend in marketing is to list all the different functions a product will do and market it as 'multi-role' or 'multi-functional'.

When we look at the Bible, we see that the Holy Spirit fulfills many roles in the spiritual development of individual Christians and Christian organizations. The Holy Spirit is very multi-role, or multi-functional. One role of the Holy Spirit is connecting God in heaven with disciples of Jesus, on Earth. And equally, another role is connecting disciples of Jesus on Earth with God the Father.

Can you see the two connecting roles – heaven to earth and earth to heaven?

Role no 1: Communicator

The reason the Holy Spirit is able to fulfill those dual connecting roles is because of a close relationship to God the Father and to Jesus.

The Apostle Paul wrote

> *"The Spirit searches all things, even the deep things of God."1 Cor 2:10*

"The Spirit searches all thing, **even the deep things of God.**" These words imply there is nothing about the nature of God that the Holy Spirit is not aware of.

During his extended teaching session about the Holy Spirit, Jesus taught the disciples that the Holy Spirit takes those thoughts that are on the heart of God, and reveals them to us

> *"the Spirit comes, who reveals the truth about God." John 16.13 (G.N)*

So that is one of the key roles or functions, of the Holy Spirit is to "**reveal**" truth to us, truth that God wants us to know. That truth is revealed to those who are open to what God's Spirit is saying.

The Apostle Paul wrote about the same process.

> *"We have ….received ….the Spirit who is from God, that we may understand what God has freely given us." 1 Cor 2:12*

That is why it is important to pray daily, "come fill me afresh Holy Spirit" because through that invitation the Holy Spirit will know we are an open channel to receive, thoughts from God.

When the Apostle John was on the Island of Patmos, he had a vision. In that vision, Jesus appeared and spoke to him repeating these words, seven times.

> *"He who has an ear (a spiritual ear) let him hear what the Spirit says to the churches." Rev 2:17 Words in brackets added.*

The context of these words are Jesus' assessment the spiritual life of seven churches in Asia-minor. Jesus commended most aspects of the life of these churches, but also pointed out some deficiencies. What is implied by these words, if any Church leadership listens to the Holy Spirit, they are hearing Jesus' plan for their church.

So a key role of the Holy Spirit is, to communicate the thoughts of God the Father, and of Jesus, to us. If the coin is flipped, we find that it is a role or ministry of the Holy Spirit to communicate our needs 'to' God and what is best for us - as we seek to do the will of God.

Paul wrote

> *"the Spirit intercedes for the saints in accordance with God's will."*
> *Rom 8:27*

The lasting imprint these Scriptures create is that the Holy Spirit is intimately involved in a two-way freeway/motorway of information between heaven, and Earth. This two-way freeway/highway of information between God in heaven and disciples of Jesus on Earth, is also suggested by what Paul wrote to the Church at Rome.

1 <u>God to disciples.</u> "For his Spirit joins with our spirit to affirm that we are God's children. Rom 8:16 NLT

2 <u>Disciples to God</u>. …"for the Spirit pleads for us believers in harmony with God's own will." Rom 8:227 NLT

Role no 2: Creator

In the first chapter of Genesis, when there was no form to the Earth, it is written

> "and the Spirit of God was hovering over the waters". Gen 1:2 (NLT)

Often in the Bible, both the Father and the Holy Spirit are pictured working in tandem. In Genesis chapter one, God is creating and the Spirit is there, "hovering over the waters". Similarly, when the angel Gabriel told Mary that she would conceive while still a virgin, both God the creator and the Holy Spirit are mentioned, in the same verse. Luke 1:35

We see throughout the pages of the Bible, that the Holy Spirit is involved in creating new life. That occurs on a large scale (with the formation of the world – universe) and on a smaller scale; when we are born anew of the Spirit or in Mary's case. With the conception of the baby Jesus.

There are other aspects to the creativity of the Holy Spirit. In Exodus 31: 1-5, God spoke to Moses and said

> "I have chosen Bezalel... and I have filled him with the Spirit of God....to engage in all kinds of craftsmanship.

The Holy Spirit is involved in inspiring men and women to create and bring to fruition all kinds of crafts, both physical and spiritual. The Holy Spirit is also involved in creating the inspiration for people to speak and write inspired words. David wrote

> "The Spirit of the Lord spoke through me, his word was on my tongue." 2 Sam 23:3

And although it is not explicit, it is implicit in Jesus' words that the Holy Spirit inspires musicians to lead us in worship. Jesus said what God was looking for, was people who would worship him "in Spirit and in truth". John 4:24.

The greatest delight God receives from worship is when it is an honest (truthful) expression of our heart and coming as a result of songs, choruses and hymns written by people inspired by the Holy Spirit, and led by musicians also inspired by the Holy Spirit.

Role no 3: Bearer of fruit

Another role of the Holy Spirit is to grow fruit in us. Jesus wanted his disciples to bear fruit, and be productive. John 15.2 & Matt 25. 1-18 Nine fruits of the Spirit are listed in Paul's letter to the Galatians, and they fall into three categories.

> **1**: *Joy and peace*, are gifts from heaven to the Christian, to help us on the way.

> **2**: *Patience, self control and faithfulness* are qualities that the Holy Spirit seeks to build into our lives so we will be fruitful and successful as Christians. If we lack self control, for example, we can make a mess of things. Likewise, if we are not patient; impatience can at times make the difference between a satisfactory or successful outcome – and an unsatisfactory or negative outcome.

> **3**: *Love*, g*oodness, kindness and gentleness*, are fruits given for the benefit of others – and the world needs people with these fruits.

These fruits are supernatural, not natural. They can be experienced, even when events are going against us or in times or turbulence or trouble. I vividly recall a Pastor from New Zealand telling our congregation about his experience on a ship called *The Wahine.* A ship that ran aground in the entrance to Wellington Harbor during a violent storm.

With the conditions being what they were, peace is the last thing that pastor on this ship, should have experienced. On that day, winds were surpassing 100 miles per hour and great damage was caused to both the vessel and houses in Wellington.

Howling winds, dark gray skies and huge waves pounding the ship; it lurched to starboard and impaled itself on rocks close to the Seatoun shoreline. Passengers were bundled into life boats. The pastor said, "As we waited our turn to board the life boats, and with the storm still raging; all along, I had an incredible peace."

These fruit are not dependent on natural causes. i.e. Some people love a particular person, because that person first loved them. Most people become happy for a while, when they have won something or have been promoted or given gifts. People enjoy peace when they go somewhere peaceful or listen to peaceful music.

By contrast, the love, joy and peace of the Holy Spirit is given to us, to help us love people who we have no natural reason to love. To have joy, even when we have no natural reason to have joy. And peace, even when things are not peaceful.

How does the fruit grow?

Some say we do nothing. All we need do is ask the Holy Spirit to fill us and the fruit will show. However, just because we have the Holy Spirit in us does not mean that we will show the fruit. That is because the Holy Spirit works in co-operation with us.

The Holy Spirit will give us the desire and even prompt us, but will never force us to show the fruits.

The fruits grow on the tree of our life to obey the prompting of the Holy Spirit to be patient, when we could have been impatient. To be gentle, when we could have been harsh in a particular situation. In other words, the Holy Spirit may prompt us and create a desire to show the fruit, but He will not force us to do or say anything.

Apart from our co-operation, other factors can influence whether we show the fruit of the Spirit. Fruit on any tree can turn bad or become damaged by hail or stunted through drought or wilt due to poisons in the soil.

So also the fruit of the Spirit in our lives can be retarded by a number of factors. The disease of unforgiveness, or bitterness, or lust, or greed, or revenge, or selfishness, or racial prejudice.

These quench the flow of the Spirit to the fruit in our lives – consequently the fruit will show signs of souring, or becoming stunted or pock-marked, like real fruit. 1Thess 5:19

Role 4: Evangelist

The Holy Spirit is not called an "Evangelist", anywhere in the Bible, but the title Evangelist is an appropriate title for the Holy Spirit. Three verses indicate why the word 'Evangelist' is appropriate.

> *"But you will receive power when the Holy Spirit comes on you; and you will be my witnesses in Jerusalem, and in all Judea and Samaria and to the ends of the earth." Acts 1:8*

A similar train of thought is found in Acts 2:17-21 where Peter is quoting the prophet Joel and talking about the Holy Spirit.

> *"For in the last day, God says, I will pour out my Spirit on all*

people,......And everyone who calls on the name of the Lord will be saved. "

Jesus at the beginning of his ministry, said

"The Spirit of the Lord is on me, because he has anointed me to <u>preach good news</u>...Luke 4.18

Can you see the connection between the Holy Spirit, and people being witnesses, being saved, and the preaching of the good news?

Where-ever, when-ever and how-ever the gospel is proclaimed, the Holy Spirit is involved. However, the work of the Holy Spirit (the Evangelist), does not end there. Jesus indicated that one role of the Holy Spirit is to convict people of their guilt in regard to sin and righteousness and also in regard to judgment. John 16:8

With evangelism, the Holy Spirit has a dual role, both with those witnessing and those who are being witnessed to.

The work of the Holy Spirit is necessary, because in the relativist age we live in. An age where people do not readily admit they are sinful people because the reasoning of our age is "What may be right for you, maybe wrong for me and what may be wrong for you, maybe right for me."

So the message of the Bible, we are all sinful people and have sinned (Rom 3:23), is not accepted easily, because that message is counter-culture. Any person can still reject the Gospel message because of their free will. But if they accept the Gospel message, it will be because of 3 factors.

1   The Gospel message has been proclaimed.

2   People listening were open enough to receive it.

3   Because the Holy Spirit was at work in their hearts and minds.

Role 5: The teacher

Another role of the Holy Spirit has, is a teacher. Speaking of the Holy Spirit, Jesus said "He will teach you and will remind you of everything I have said." John 14:26

But even though someone reads the Bible or listens to inspired teachers, they will not necessarily understand it, unless the Holy Spirit reveals it to them. John 16:13 There are different ways the Holy Spirit can teach us –

by prompting, speaking, revealing, inspiring, and through different avenues. It could be a book, or a sermon, or the example of someone's life; but primarily through the bible.

It is necessary to have the Holy Spirit to help us understand the Bible because even though we may read it, we will not understand it fully until the Holy Spirit "highlights" or reveals a particular truth. See John 16:13.

The Apostle Paul wrote about an example of revelation

> *"No, we speak of God's secret wisdom,.... A wisdom that. "None of the rulers of this age understood it".... 1 Cor 2:8*

Then in verse ten Paul explains who understood it and why.

> *"but God has revealed it to us by his Spirit."*

The Holy Spirit has down through the centuries, taken the Gospel message which to natural minds does not make sense, and revealed it to people who are open to the power of its' truth. That principle applies to the rest of Scripture as well - and even other truth that he, the Counselor (the Holy Spirit) wants to point out to us.

Role 6: The Reminder/Recaller

Another role that Jesus indicated the Holy Spirit would fulfill, is to remind the disciples of Jesus' words - at an appropriate point in time. Jesus said of the Holy Spirit

> "He will remind you of everything I have said." John 14:26

I appreciated the ability of the Holy Spirit to remind me of the words of the Bible decades ago, when I was traveling around Europe on my own. After spending 3 weeks in England, I traveled through Germany, then made my way to Sweden and then back down to Denmark. From Denmark, I flew down to Czechoslovakia as it was known in those days, and then on to Israel.

When I was flying down to Czechoslovakia, I thought to myself 'For the most part since leaving England twelve days ago, I have been on my own and have been talking to myself."

I knew just a smattering of German to help me when in Germany, but knew no Danish or Swedish to help me in those countries. I got by, by pointing to things I wanted to get. Before leaving for Europe I had purchased phrase books to help me communicate in those countries. To my horror, when traveling from Germany to Sweden, I found that the books with Swedish and Danish were missing.

Now I am a person who likes times when I am not with people and on my own, but equally I like times of normal conversation with familiar people, even if the talk is only about the weather.

Even though I had only been on a diet of normal conversation for twelve days, by the time I was flying down to the then communist country of Czechoslovakia on a plane of the state airline, I admitted to myself that for the first time in my life I was feeling lonely, and not enjoying it.

I knew no Danish, the country I had just left, and nothing of the Czech language, the country I was going to. I also contemplated my next stop after Czechoslovakia, which was Israel, and knew I would have to find English speaking people there also, if I was to converse with anybody.

So I was essentially alone, though surrounded by millions of people, whose language I could not understand. As I thought about being alone and on the other side of the World, I was flying at perhaps 14,000 feet and 10,000 miles from my home country (and feeling every mile of it), I began to long for those regular conversations you have with familiar people.

The sense of being alone and so far from home was highlighted by the political divides at that time in world history. The World was divided into the Communist bloc, Capitalist Bloc and the non-aligned World.

As I flew along, I reminded myself that I was flying on a 'communist airline' and traveling to a communist country.

While these thoughts were circulating about being on a 'communist plane' the fact that I had talked very little with others for the last twelve days, I reminded myself that this pattern was going to continue until I got home.

The words flashed across my mind, as clearly as the no smoking lights going on in an aircraft,

> *'or where we are - high above the sky'*

Initially I had no idea where those words came from or why. Did those words come from a poem, or were they a quote by somebody famous, or were they from the Bible? After a while I began to think that they were from the Bible, and from Psalm 139. The part where it says,

> *"Where can I go from your Spirit, where can I flee from your presence? Where can I flee from your presence? If I go up to the heavens, you are there; Psa 139: 7-8*

Not having a Bible with me, I concluded that these words came from Psalm 139 and that the Holy Spirit had brought these words back to my memory, to remind me that no matter where I was or how far from home I was, God was there. He knew where I was and, he understood.

A month later, when I got home, I found out that the words, *'Or where we are, high in the sky'* came from the book of Romans – and were from Living Bible paraphrase. The preceding words were,

> "For I am convinced that nothing can ever separate us from his love. Our fears for today, our worries about tomorrow, or where we are - high above the sky...." Rom 8:38 & 39 (Living Bible)

When I was reminded of those words by the Holy Spirit, it did not matter that I could not pick which part of the Bible they came from or the version of the Bible. I got the message. I was being reminded of the truth of Psalm 139 by the Holy Spirit, that though I was I was on other side of the globe (about 10,000 miles from home) and moving among people whose languages I could not understand, this was not unfamiliar territory to either the Holy Spirit, or to God the Father. Nor were these people unfamiliar to him.

The Holy Spirit is not restricted to Scripture, to highlight truth. He is after all, the Spirit of truth - all truth. So it could be from any version of the Bible, or the words of a book or a chorus or hymn that the Holy Spirit may use to communicate a truth he wants us to remember.

A an example, the Holy Spirit has brought this truth back to my memory a number of times. These words are from a short poem based on Jesus' teaching. Matthew 6:25-34 When I first heard this little poem, I thought. 'How quaint'. That is a simple little ditty that perhaps helps others, but it is not something I care to or need to, remember.

However the Holy Spirit is wiser, and has brought the words of that short poem back to my memory, a number of times. Times when I have let life's problems and challenges get out of perspective, and I have chosen to worry, instead of trusting God for my future, and live, one day at a time!

> *"Worry not over the future, the present is all thou hast. The future will soon be present, the present will soon be past."*

Amongst the two most quoted sayings of angels are, "do not fear" and amongst the sayings of Jesus, are the words; "do not worry". They (Father/Son/Holy Spirit) know us human beings, better than we do, so it is sometimes necessary for them to remind us of God's protection and provision with the words such as, "do not fear" and "do not worry". For as Jesus said, "God will take care of tomorrow" – and so – "live one day at a time".

Those quaint words, couched in Shakespearean English, contain a truth I needed to hear from time to time and perhaps we all need to hear, from time to time.

Role 7: Foreteller of the future

This section called 'The Holy Spirit - Foreteller of the future', was not originally part of the script, but was added as result of the Holy Spirit foretelling me about one aspect of a disaster that was about to occur in the city of

Christchurch, New Zealand where I was living in at the time. That experience reminded me that the Holy Spirit knows ahead of time what is going to happen, which for some is uncomfortable.

In both testaments of the bible, people in whom the Holy Spirit lived, sometimes prophesied future events. Isaiah who lived about 700 years before Jesus, predicted that the Messiah would suffer. Most of the major and minor prophets, foretold coming events.

After Joseph explained the dream of the Pharaoh indicating there would be seven years of famine in Egypt, the Pharaoh exclaimed

> "Can we find anyone like this man,
> one in whom is the spirit of God?"
> Gen 41:38

Elijah prophesied that there would be a famine in Israel (1 King 17:1) and Elisha his successor asked

> "Let me inherit a double portion of
> your spirit," 2 Kings 2:9

After Elisha had inherited a double portion of the Holy Spirit, he too was able to predict future events. After a long siege of the city of Samaria, Elisha prophesied that on the following day, there would be an abundance of food. 2 Kings 7:1-20

Moving on through the Bible to the time of Daniel. During the reign of King Nebuchadnezzar the king had a dream about a large tree that was cut down. The King's astrologers were not able to interpret his dream, so the King asked Daniel to interpret it. King Nebuchadnezzar exclaimed

> "Belshazzar (Daniel's Babylonian name), chief of the magicians, I know the spirit of the holy gods is in you, and no mystery is too hard for you…..Daniel 4:9

Daniel went on to explain that the cutting down of the tree and a stump remaining symbolized a time when King Nebuchadnezzar's reign would come to an end and then after a period of seven years, it would be restored.

Examples of the Holy Spirit giving God's people insight into the future, continue in the New Testament. In Luke's gospel for example, we read

> "Now there was a man in Jerusalem called Simeon, who was righteous and devout. He was waiting for the consolation of Israel,

and the Holy Spirit was upon him. It had been revealed to him by the Holy Spirit that he would not die before he had seen the Lord's Christ. Moved by the Spirit, he went to the temple courts. When the parents brought in the child Jesus to do for him what the custom of the law required, Simeon took him in his arms and praised God..."
Luke 2:25-28 (NIV)

Jesus was filled with the Holy Spirit and was able to predict the future events. See Matthew chapter 24. After the Church was established, we see examples of the same Holy Spirit, helping Christians understand the future. The Holy Spirit was on a prophet named Agabus who predicted a severe famine in that part of the world. Acts 11:28. The Holy Spirit warned Paul that he would face hardships in the future. Acts 20:23.

Prophecy is a gift of the Holy Spirit (I Cor 12:10) so we should not be surprised by all these examples. People in whom the Holy Spirit lived; were given an insight into the future. Joseph, Isaiah, Elijah, Elisha, Daniel, Simeon, Jesus, Agabus, Paul.

The Holy Spirit gives knowledge of future events to inform God's people to prepare them. The Father/Son and Holy Spirit are the 'same' yesterday, today and forever.

For me, a good lesson from the recent devastating earthquake in Christchurch, New Zealand is that our ultimate security is not what we 'think' will provide security, but in God. God provided for us wonderfully after that earthquake through people and circumstances. The words of King David were relevant to that experience.

> "Even though I walk through the valley of the shadow of death, *even there* your hand will lead me... Psa 23.

We do not need to fear any future difficult times because the Father/Son and Holy Spirit already know about them and have gone there in advance.

Role 8: Convicts us of Sin and righteousness – John 16:8

It is one of the roles of the Holy Spirit to convict people of their sin, and about what is right. Perhaps some readers are thinking "I can pass on this section of the chapter because I haven't robbed a bank or murdered people or ..."

Those who walk in the Spirit find that it is not just the 'big things' of life the Holy Spirit speaks to us about. Sometimes it is the little things, the seeming insignificant thoughts, words and actions, that we so easily justify. An example from my own life from that earthquake period of my life.

Prior to the February earthquake, I asked an outboard shop to repair a minor part of my motor. I found that the only way they could repair the minor problem was to supply a whole section of the motor, which was far more expensive than I had anticipated. In fact I only just had enough in my bank account to pay for the part and labor. When I picked up the motor, I talked with the man at the shop about why the problem occurred and he recommended I buy an ancillary piece of equipment, only costing $17.

I had just cleaned out my bank account paying for the motor, so did not have a spare $17. The man in the shop said. "Here is the part. Pay for it next time you are passing."

That is what I intended to do and kept the outer cover for the $17 part in my car as a reminder to pay the shop when I next passed. Christmas came and went, and each time I saw that outer cover with the bar-code on it, I thought to myself "I must put call in and pay the $17, or put a check in the mail."

After the earthquake we shifted to another city. I began to reason "It doesn't matter now about a mere $17? The business has probably been damaged by the earthquake and because businesses in that part of the city have been affected, the business may well be closed by now so I do not need to worry about paying the $17." Further I reasoned.

"I can't remember the name of the shop nor the address so there's no need to worry about sending a check"

But! Somehow I knew in my spirit that the Holy Spirit wanted me to honor my word, and repay this man's trust in me. However, I had the Holy Spirit cornered. I could say I can't remember the name of the business, or it's address.

Guess what, about the time I was telling the Holy Spirit that I can't remember the name of the company or it's address, I turned to a Christian radio station that I do not normally listen to and heard the name and address of that company in an ad. Quickly after that, I mailed the check.

It was not a big sin, forgetting to pay the $17, but if we are to open to what Holy Spirit is saying He may prompt us to return something, repay something, forgive someone.

The Holy Spirit does not condemn us, but may gently convict us of something that may seem very minor, but is a sin or unrighteousness. If I were to justify not paying the $17, then it would be an easy step to justify not paying a bigger sum.

It is to the credit of Holy Spirit, that He just quietly and persistently let me know in my spirit that he wanted me to honor my word.

That is the wonderful Holy Spirit we Christians have as our helper, guide and teacher of the truth.

We win and others win when we are open to what the Holy Spirit is saying to us or prompting us to do. Next time we may on the receiving end of someone doing something for us that the Holy Spirit has prompted them to do.

Chapter 5

The Divine Person

During my first twenty years as a committed Christian, I thought the Holy Spirit was either some kind of divine electric current, or a divine vapor that filled people. Jesus promised the first disciples they would "receive power" when the Holy Spirit came on them (Acts 1:8) and in the book of Ephesians, the Apostle Paul wrote

"be filled with the Spirit." Eph 5:18

It was only when I read a Bible study that included many verses about the personal nature of the Holy Spirit, that I realized the Holy Spirit was much more than an inanimate power or vapor. It was obvious from this study that The Holy Spirit is a person. Or as I sometimes call Him, a *divine personal being.* Understanding that the Holy Spirit is a *divine personal being*, was a significant stepping stone in my Christian journey.

Jesus taught that the Holy Spirit is a divine personal being. See John chapters 14-16. Before his crucifixion Jesus took the disciples aside to teach them what would be necessary for them, once He was gone. During that pre-crucifixion talk, Jesus frequently used the personal pronoun, 'He' of the Holy Spirit, indicating that the Holy Spirit is a personal being. See John 14:16

In what we now call the great commission, Jesus commanded the disciples to go into all the world

> "baptizing them in the name of the Father and of the Son and of the Holy Spirit". Matt 28:19

These words could be rendered . . . baptizing them in the *names* of the Father and of the Son and of the Holy Spirit. (italics added)

Or

. . . baptizing them in the *name* of the Father and the *name* of the Son and the *name* of the

Holy Spirit.

In the great commission, three divine personal beings are named, on of them being the Holy Spirit.

There are other references in the Bible that indicate why the Holy Spirit should be considered *a divine personal being,* and not just a force or power. Consider some of these verses.

The Spirit has a mind

> The Holy Spirit teaches people John 14:26
>
> The Holy Spirit reminds people John 14: 26
>
> The Holy Spirit speaks. He said "set apart for me, Barnabas and Saul…. Acts 13:2

The Holy Spirit has emotions

> The Spirit loves Rom 15:30
>
> Do not grieve the Holy Spirit Eph 4:30
>
> The Spirit groans Rom 8:26

Only personal beings have emotions, love, grieve or groan.

Other Scriptures that imply the Holy Spirit is a divine personal being, are

> "that you have lied to the Holy Spirit" Acts 5:3

> "and the fellowship of the Holy Spirit be with you all." 2 Cor 13:13

> "but anyone who blasphemes against the Holy Spirit will not be forgiven" Luke 12:10

You cannot 'lie' to an impersonal source of power. You cannot have fellowship with a vapor but you can have fellowship with a personal being. You cannot blaspheme an electrical current, but you can blaspheme someone, who is a person.

The mind of the Spirit

Among the characteristics of a person is that they have emotions and a mind. Paul wrote

> "And he who searches our hearts, knows the *mind* of the Spirit. Rom 8:27

So what is this 'mind' of the Spirit? To understand the mind of the Holy Spirit and the intelligence he has, it will be necessary to use our imagination.

Using our imagination:

> Anyone who considers the Bible, God's word to us, will believe that any promise in the Bible, is a promise to

every disciple of Jesus, where-ever they may live in the World. Let us apply that understanding to just one promise Jesus made about the Holy Spirit.

"He will teach you much and remind you of all that I have taught you." John 14:26.

To understand the amazing mind the Holy Spirit, it is necessary to consider the implications of that promise Jesus made. For the Holy Spirit to fulfill that one promise, to teach or remind each person of Jesus words, means he must know every language of the world as there are likely to be Christians in every language group in the world.

There are approximately 6000 recognized languages or subgroups of languages in the world. So the Holy Spirit must know all of them to be able to teach or remind any Christian who speaks any of the world's 6,000 languages.

That is some undertaking as anyone who has tried to learn another language or languages, will realize. Most languages are 'distinctly' different. The different languages use different words different grammar and different syntax to describe the same object or idea, as the following example illustrates. The sentence in

English;

> "I always play tennis on Monday
> with my friend."

would be re-arranged like this by someone
speaking German

> "Am Sontag spiele ich immer mit
> meine Freund tennis." - On Monday
> play I always with my friend tennis.

It is noticeable that different words are used
and they are arranged differently. That is true
of 'every' language. To the north of Australia
are the Torres Islands. On those islands they
speak, Torres Island Creole. in Torres Island
Creole, Matthew 12:46 reads

> Seimtaim nau wen Zizas I bin tok
> po dem bigmob pipol de, mada ane
> ol bala Zizas I bin sane tok lo
> wanman go po singaut Zizas kam
> ausaid po demla bikoz dempla
> wande tok po em.

German, Torres Island Creole, are two of the
6,000 languages the Holy Spirit must know to
fulfill that one promise of Jesus.

In Hebrew there are no consonants, they read
from right to left. There are many different
alphabets in use today. And the Holy Spirit
must know each of them.

To fulfill that one promise of Jesus, the Holy Spirit must know every word of each language, their alphabet and the appropriate sentence construction.

The size of the task the Holy Spirit has, is not only determined by the number of languages, but by the number of Christians in this World. There are an estimated 1.8 billion Christians in the world,.

To fulfill that one promise of Jesus, the Holy Spirit must know every language of the world, and also every Christian and their unique circumstances. For instance, a Scripture that is appropriate for Christian no. 98,016,783; is not the right Scripture verse for Christian no. 723,859,102 or Christian no 3,450, 965.

I gave an example in an earlier chapter where I wrote about how the Holy Spirit brought back to my memory the words *"or where we are; high in the sky."* The circumstances were, I was flying at 14,000 ft in a plane of a communist airline on the other side of the World.

To remind me of those words, the Holy Spirit had to be tracking me round the globe, and know my thoughts about being alone. Then He searched through the 31,000 verses of the different translations of the Bible I had read, to find just the right words.

So 20 years into my Christian journey my thinking about the Holy Spirit changed. From considering Him an almost irrelevant and mysterious force, to an attitude of enormous respect.

We Christians can be at one extreme or the other. Either we are unfamiliar with who the Holy Spirit is, and treat Him like some kind of current or vapor. Or we are at the other extreme, and believe we know all there is to know about the Holy Spirit, and treat the Spirit of God as if He is merely a light switch that we turn on and off; at will.

The personality of the Spirit

Apart from intelligence, the other characteristic of a person, is that they have emotions. In both testaments of the Bible, the word 'grieve' is used in connection with the Holy Spirit. Isa 63.10 & Eph 4.30. In Isaiah, the word grieve was used in connection with the actions of the people of Israel. Isaiah contrasted the love and mercy of God to the Jewish people's rebellion. The Jewish people ignored the truth God gave them and the Holy Spirit grieved, as they went their own way.

This word 'grieve' is also found in connection with the Holy Spirit in the New Testament. The context of the word 'grieve' in the book of Ephesians is about contrasting words and actions. In that letter, the Apostle Paul wrote about a series of words and actions that the Holy Spirit rejoices over, and others that the Holy Spirit grieves over. The words and actions that 'grieve' the Holy Spirit, include:

- unwholesome words

- speaking falsely

- stealing

- impurity

- lust

The words and actions that please the Holy Spirit, include:

- helpful words

- truthful words

- honest work

- righteousness

- holiness.

The Holy Spirit, being a divine personal being also radiates positive emotions like joy. Luke wrote

> "Jesus, full of joy through the Holy Spirit" Luke 10.21

Then there are the fruits of the Spirit

- love

- joy

- peace

- patience

- kindness

- goodness

- faithfulness

- gentleness and

- self control

      - Gal 5:22

What most Christians do not think about when they read that list of fruits, is that the Holy Spirit must have those fruits as part of his nature, to be able to give them to us.

To make that point clearer, Galatians 5:22 has been rewritten

> *If you have the Holy Spirit in your life, He will give you His 'very own nature' - the fruits of: love, joy, peace, patience, kindness, goodness, faithfulness,*

gentleness and self control.

Fellowship with the Holy Spirit

Paul's final words to the Church at Corinth

> "... and the fellowship of the Holy Spirit be with you all" 2 Cor 13.14

More often and not we Christians miss out on fellowship with the Holy Spirit because in our worship services we want to be singing all time or hear someone speaking, when ideally we will allow for times of silence for fellowship with the Holy Spirit. Perhaps we are afraid of silence?

There are several conclusions we can draw from the fact that the Holy Spirit is a divine, personal being. When I first realized that the Holy Spirit was not just an impersonal force but a divine personal being, I asked myself. "Can I pray directly to him and ask him things? Or must I ask God the Father to convey my requests to the Holy Spirit?"

There is Scriptural precedent for asking God to send his Holy Spirit but does that mean we cannot pray directly to the Holy Spirit? Eventually I came to the conclusion that because the Holy Spirit is a divine personal being, we must be able to pray directly to him.

Hymn writers of the past and chorus writers of

today have come to same conclusion and address the Holy Spirit directly. The words of one hymn for example are

"Come Holy Spirit, our hearts inspire"

and the words of a contemporary chorus also addresses the Holy Spirit directly.

"Spirit of the Living God, fall afresh on me".

There is another conclusion we can draw from the realization that the Holy Spirit is a divine personal being. For some reason I thought of the trinity like this. When-ever the affairs of the Church or events on the Earth were discussed in heaven. God the Father and Jesus the Son, would meet together in the throne-room; and discuss these affairs and events, while the Holy Spirit was out in a back-room, waiting to be summoned, and told what decisions the other two had made. When I realized that the Holy Spirit is a divine personal being with great knowledge, power and intelligence, I realized that the Holy Spirit would be there as an equal partner in these round-table discussions. That equality is implied by the Great Commission. Matt 28:29.

This Holy Spirit embodies a number of factors. A memory and intelligence, far beyond the most powerful computer in existence. An intimate knowledge of, billions of human beings. Emotions like joy and grief and yet, most amazing of all. He wants 'fellowship' with people like you and I. He wants to share the fruits He has. He wants to guide us and teach us God's ways and God's truth. He wants to touch us for our good and distribute the love of God into our hearts.

Chapter 6

Led By The Spirit

"...for all who are led by the Spirit of God are children of God." Rom 8.14 NLT

The context of this verse are two choices we have in life. The choices of being led by our sinful nature or led, by the Spirit of God. Every day we have to make choices and about what we say and do and think. Further, as a Christians, it is equally important not only what we say and do and think, but 'how' we do anything and equally important are our motives for doing anything.

There is guidance about what we will say or

do, or think during any given day in Romans chapter 12, while and our motives and various ways the Holy Spirit can impact our lives are spelt out in Romans 8:1-27. Included amongst words found in Romans chapter 8 is this word - "Controlled".

In those verses, Paul wrote that we can be controlled by our sinful nature (i.e. people who are forever chasing wealth for the status value, sexual encounters; have addictions to gambling or drugs or alcohol; are controlled by those forces). Others are controlled by their hatred or a desire for revenge. That is one side of the coin.

The other side of the coin, and one that Paul advocates is that we be controlled by the Holy Spirit! As soon as I write "controlled", some are going to say "I don't want to be controlled by any person or being, including the Holy Spirit." That reaction comes from the desire of most human beings to be independent of - and not reliant on; any other person or being.

The benefits of being controlled and led by the Holy Spirit are found in Romans Chapter 8:

- Set free form the law of sin and death 8:1-2

- Experience "life and peace". 8:6

- Please God (implied) 8:9

- Helps us put to death our sinful nature. 8:13

- Considered God's children. 8:14

- Creates a desire in us to call God "Abba, Father" 8:15

- Helps us in our weaknesses. 8:26

- Helps us to pray for solutions to any situation. 8:26

It is implied in these verses and other verses in the Bible, that to be controlled by our sinful nature results in 'living death' and a troubled conscience; while to be controlled by the Holy Spirit results in "life and peace".

Staying with the word "controlled", several other points need to be made. Our relationships with the Father, Son and Holy Spirit; is always "voluntary." They will never coerce us to do anything against our will They want us to desire what they have to offer. They want us to invite them into our lives. The picture of Jesus knocking at the door of our lives (Revelation 3:20) is symbolic of the invitation that the Father/Son and Holy Spirit wait for us to give.

Because they never force us to do anything, we have to 'desire' to be controlled by the Holy Spirit. When we invite the Holy Spirit to lead us, He wants to be the controlling factor in everything we do or say or think, and examine our motives and attitudes.

Let me illustrate that last point about motives, through a brief parable. I will use myself in this parable as I do not want to blacken anyone else's character.

Say I decide to give some money to someone who needs it. However, though it is not initially obvious to the person or anyone else, I have a motive for giving this money which is "I want something in return for this money – which is my real reason for offering the money, in the first place."

Assuming that I want the Holy Spirit to lead me, the Holy Spirit will look at my motives for giving this money, he will quietly suggest "You are really giving that money, primarily for 'your' benefit rather than the benefit of the other person."

We all need people who are honest with us, and we also need the "the Spirit of truth" to be honest with us. Paul offers a hint that the Holy Spirit controlled him in this way. He wrote

> "I speak the truth in Christ – I am not lying, my conscience confirms it in the Holy Spirit." Rom 9:1

That is 'one' way the Holy Spirit leads us, by being a gentle but honest friend whose motive is to help us be true sons and daughters of God.

When we are led by the Holy Spirit we do not lose our personality or our ability to think clearly and make good decisions. The Holy Spirit values our unique personality.

Being led by the Holy Spirit helps us achieve one of the goals of Christian life – to do the "will of God." It could be said that "The Spirit prays in line with God's will." See Rom 8:27

How To Be Led By the Spirit of God

The "how to" is not as important as our attitude to being led by the Spirit of God, because the Holy Spirit often leads different Christians in different ways. The starting point is:

- The Holy Spirit wants to lead us for our good, to make us more like Jesus, to make us effective children of God.

- We all have spiritual antennas and all we need do is tune our antenna into the Holy Spirit's wavelength.

The Holy Spirit can guide or lead us in a number of ways:

- Speak to us in plain English or our native tongue

- Speak to us without speaking - sometimes we just know!

- Speak to us in a vision

- The Holy Spirit can prompt us, inspire us and motivate us. Any number of sermons, songs, books, works of art and crafts have been created at the inspiration of the Holy Spirit.

Several examples from the Bible. When the Holy Spirit began to work in Samson, we read. "The Spirit of the Lord began to stir him".... Judges 13:25, and Paul wrote, "And now compelled by the Spirit, I am going to Jerusalem,"...Acts 20:25

Wesley L Duewel wrote

"God gives many practical inner suggestions and moral and holy impressions. These are given you by the Holy Spirit. The Spirit's voice occasionally comes as a sudden impulse or restraint. Often, however, it comes as a gradually deepening conviction. "

Let God Guide You Daily p105 (Duewel

Literature Trust)

Usually Christians are aware it is the Holy Spirit inspiring them, but sometimes they may not be aware and it is only by looking back that they will say "I am sure it was the Holy Spirit who was motivating and inspiring me."

The leading of the Holy Spirit can be found in 'every' area of our lives. Ed Cole wrote about a business man who felt prompted to check the details of a building his firm had just signed to build, and found an error in the plans. By recognizing the error, it saved his firm legal action once the building was complete. Another example.

My wife knows what it is to be led by the Holy Spirit when it comes to buying clothes for our family. Because of the financial limits placed on her purchases by our family budget, she prays "Holy Spirit, lead me." So the leading of the Holy Spirit can be in business matters, personal matters and spiritual matters.

The Holy Spirit may prompt us to pray about a person or a situation. Another time He may remind us about a particular verse in the Bible that He wants us to remember. The Holy Spirit may prompt us to do good for someone.

His leading may be to do with business

matters, any aspect of Church life, the needs of others, or about our personal needs. There is no such thing as the separation of the 'secular' and 'sacred', with the Holy Spirit.

When a person is led by the Spirit, their thoughts and actions are directed to do something close to the heart of God. Those who obey the Spirits promptings find far greater satisfaction than from any other source. Said Paul,

> "the mind controlled by the Spirit is
> life and peace." Rom 8: 6 (NIV)

Being led by the Spirit may also involve doing things our natural mind may argue against and we may think that if we obey the Spirit's prompting we will look foolish. Philip was asked by an angel to go to the road between Jerusalem and Gaza. When Philip was by the road he noticed this important Ethiopian official coming along in his chariot. Then the Spirit said to Philip

> "Go to that chariot and stay near it."
> Acts 8:29.

It is possible Philip thought "If I go and run by that chariot, I will look silly or I could be rebuffed by the attendants of this important official." Philip was not told to go to the

Chariot and evangelize that important person, but urged by the Spirit to go and run beside it.

Being led by the Spirit is dependent on these factors implicit in Romans 8.14

1. That it is possible to be led by the Spirit.

2. That God wants us to be led by the Spirit.

3. That we have to desire to be led by the Spirit.

4. That we have an attitude of wanting to learn how to be led by the Holy Spirit.

If we are led by the Spirit, it can become a normal, natural, everyday experience. The leading of the Spirit may be for the purpose of going on a missionary journey, but for most Christians, His guidance will be about everyday things.

Learning to be led by the Spirit
Probably the three most over-looked words in the Bible are 'I have learned' Phil 4:11 The context of those words are "...for I have learned to be content in whatever the circumstances." Paul did not come into this life, 'programmed' to be content in whatever circumstances he found himself. He had to 'learn' to be content.

No Christian is programmed from birth to be led by the Spirit of God, nor can it be taught in school. We can only learn by our own experience, sometimes by trial and error. Paul told the elders of the Church of Ephesus.

> "And now compelled by the Spirit, I am going to Jerusalem, not knowing what will happen to me there." Acts 20:22

Where and how did Paul learn to be "compelled" by the Spirit? It was not during his training as a Pharisee. Perhaps it was during the years he spent in Arabia, tent making and doing other ordinary jobs?

As I look back on life, I see ways that I have learnt to obey the leading of the Spirit.

Amongst the lessons I have learned, if the Holy Spirit wants me to do something, that impression will not go away. Also, if something is troubling me in my spirit day after day, then the Holy Spirit is asking me to reconsider the method being used or my involvement in a particular activity.

As an example, between 20 and 26yrs old, I was heavily involved in long distance running. I was the under-19 yrs champion in my country over both 5000 meters on the track and cross-county. So as an adult, there was every reason to continue training hard with hopes of success, and perhaps of representing my country as a senior. I believed then as I do now, that people should use their God-given talents.

As I struggled to be successful as a senior athlete, I wondered why I was not fulfilling the promise shown as a junior athlete because of all the hard work I was putting in. I did not know that a piano shifting accident at the age of nineteen had dislocated my spine so that I could never be as successful in adult grades while my spine was twisted.

It was not till I was 38 that a chiropractor analyzed my problem correctly. I knew my body had taken a sharp jerk as I tried to catch the falling piano but in the thinking of a teenager, thought my spine would act like a rubber band and would automatically wind back into place.

With dreams of being a successful senior runner, I put in time and effort running 100 miles (160 km) a week, endeavoring to use the gift God had given me. By putting in that constant effort I was picking up places in national events and was either first or second in local events. I have a scrap book full of clippings with my name and photos from newspapers.

However, over a period of months in the mid to late twenties, I considered the whole situation. I was still getting my name in print in the local newspapers, but my questioning revolved around these thoughts. Success in athletics or any sport, requires a lot of time and energy and I had to ask. Is the amount of time and energy required justified?

I was often physically and mentally tired and being tired most of the time; which meant I could not give one hundred percent to my work, or Church. There was a deep unhappiness in my spirit about putting the amount energy and time into a sport as an unpaid amateur (today I could have applied for Government sponsorship) which drastically limited the amount of time and energy I had for important things like work, people and church. And there was no time, for courting my future wife.

There was no clear voice at this time, just an unhappiness in my spirit about the large amount of time and energy I was investing in Sport for reasonable success. At that time, I understood what John's words about Jesus. He wrote

> "Jesus was troubled in his spirit"
> John 13:21

After a period of time, I decided that I had to pull out of active involvement in running. It was only after I had been obedient to that prompting of the spirit and ceased active involvement in running, that the rationale for the Spirits' prompting came to mind. It was the words of a hymn.

> "This worlds empty glory is costing me too dear."

My name, continually being in the newspaper was good for the ego, but it was coming at a price - and the price was not worth it, which is what the Holy Spirit wanted me to see.

P.S: In the immediate period after giving up competitive running, I met my wife – and have enjoyed over three decades of happy marriage.

Another example of bing led by the Spirit. A number of years ago I clearly remember being prompted by the Spirit to do the dishes when it was not my turn. Possibly some readers have decided they do not want to be led by the Spirit.

There is, I suspect, a connection between being willing to be led by the Spirit in the seemingly small and insignificant matters of life, and being led by the Holy Spirit to do much more significant, and noticeable matters. Said Jesus to two of the servants in the parable of the talents,

> "You have been faithful with a few things.. but later was to add, "For to everyone who has will be given more." Matt 25:21& 29

Being led by the Spirit often involves choices between the way we want to go and the way the Spirit wants to lead. This is a choice between our desires and the desires of the Spirit. Between the things that will satisfy our lower nature and flesh and the higher nature where the Spirit lives. Rom 8: 1-14

Being led by the Spirit is not hard, it is very simple! What makes being led by the Spirit a challenge for some, is its simplicity! For some, being led by the Spirit will go against the grain of our modern life-style i.e. We live in a push-button age where pushing the appropriate button causes something to happen, straight away. But with the leading of the Spirit, sometimes we may have to wait until He gives the green light.

Even if you have been led by the Spirit many times before and are confident of the Spirit's leading; do not rest on your laurels for there is always more, and always today's opportunities and tomorrow's opportunities.

There are fresh pages of the book of Acts waiting to be written about Christians who are open to be lead by the Holy Spirit. Old Simeon who was called righteous and devout, was still being led by the Holy Spirit, at the end of his life. Luke 2: 25-28

Being led by the wrong party.
New Christians in particular may be a concerned that they could be led by the wrong spirit. It is helpful to be aware of that possibility. Satan has been, and always will be, opposed to anything God does and prefers that people to be either, neutral in spiritual matters, or to listen to his voice. He started this practice of attempting to misdirect the first humans in the garden of Eden and will continue to do so till he is chained up at the end of this era. That makes being led by the spirit a little more difficult because we have to learn to distinguish between who is attempting to lead us and our own thoughts and desires.

For those who are worried that Satan's representatives might attempt to misdirect them (as if it were the leading of the Holy

Spirit) the Bible offers some clues about distinguishing between the two sources of guidance. The devil and his colleagues are 'restless'. Job Chapter 1 and Luke 11.24 They cannot bring peace when they speak or when they prompt a person. If you are being troubled by an 'urgent, nagging' thought or voice, I would be wary about its source. By contrast, peace is a natural attribute of all three members of the trinity. Of God Phil 4:7, of Jesus John 14:27 and the Holy Spirit. Gal 5:22

The prompting of the Spirit may be regular, but not nagging. It will be in the nature of the words of the prophet Isaiah"

> "in quietness and confidence shall be your strength." Isa 30:15

There is another check. The leading of the Spirit will not go against any moral command of Scripture. You will never be led to steal, have an affair, murder or take revenge. The leading of the Holy Spirit will always align with Scripture.

> *"He who has an ear, let him hear what the Spirit says to the Churches." Rev 2:7*

Chapter 7

The Gifts of The Spirit

The main teaching in the Bible about the gifts of the Spirit, are found in the book of First Corinthians, chapters 12 to 14. But for now let us take a closer look at the record of the Holy Spirit, throughout the Bible. The Bible tells us that God does not change (James 1:17) and that Jesus remains the same, yesterday and today and forever. Heb 13:8. The Bible does not say categorically that the Holy Spirit has always been the same, but it is a reasonable assumption, for He is called 'the eternal Spirit'. Hebrews 9:14

The word 'eternal' implies that the Holy Spirit

has always been the same, and existed long before human beings came on the scene.

Although the disciples saw the Holy Spirit in the form of a dove at Jesus' baptism, and in the form of flames of fire during the feast of Pentecost, which were new revelations of the Holy Spirit, most other activities of the Holy Spirit in the New Testament were not new.

Characteristics of the Holy Spirit, common to both Testaments

Characteristics	Old Testament	Jesus Ministry	New Testament Church
Boldness	Judges 6:34	Matt 7:28	Acts 2:4&14
Prophecy	1 Sam 10:6	Mark 10:33&34	Acts 11:28
Healing	2Kings 5:14 **	Matt 8:14-17	Acts 5:15
Dead Raised	2 Kings 4: 32-35	John 11:38-44	Acts 20:9-10#

Characteristics	Old Testament	Jesus Ministry	New Testament Church
Spirit given to a group	Num 11:17	John 20:22	Acts 8:15
Spirit poured out	Isa 32:15		Acts 2:17
Grieve Holy Spirit	Isa 63:10		Eph 4:30

Unique to one Testament

Gives skills at craft work Exod 31:1-5

Ability to interpret dreams Dan 4:8

Ability to speak in language of angels 1 Cor 13:1

Ability to speak in foreign languages Acts 2:4

We can see from the above examples that of virtually every activity of the Holy Spirit in the New Testament, there were similar examples in the Old Testament. Because the Holy Spirit is the same, we can assume that He has, 'always been the giver of gifts'. The examples below, illustrate that point.

Gifts listed 1 Cor 12. 8-10

Characteristics	Old Testament	Jesus Ministry	New Testament Church
Knowledge	2 Kings 5:25&26	Luke 5: 4-6	Acts 5:3
Miracles	2 Kings 4:38-44	Matt 8:23-27	Acts 5:12
Wisdom	Deut 34:9	Matt 22:22	Acts 6:3
Faith	2 Chron 20:14-20	Matt 8:5-13	Acts 11:24

Characteristics	New Testament Church
Ability to speak in language of angels	1 Cor 13:1
Ability to speak in foreign languages	Acts 2:4
Praying in different tongues	1 Cor 1
Interpretation of tongues	1 Cor 14

* Jesus was filled with the Holy Spirit Luke 4.14

** Elisha was filled with the Holy Spirit

> \# Paul associated miracles with the presence of the Holy Spirit. Gal 3.5

From these parallel lists, we can see that the Holy Spirit has *always* been, the giver of gifts. In the Old Testament, those who had the Holy Spirit on them were able to prophecy, do miracles, heal people; some had supernatural knowledge and raised the dead.

Jesus also, once the power of the Holy Spirit came on him did all these things. It was the same in the New Testament Church, and in the period after the twelve died. St Augustine's book, City of God, written 300 years after the time of the Apostles, is full of miracles.

During the Dark Ages, teachings about the gifts of the Spirit, largely disappeared from the Church. However that was not God's plan. In God's plan, the gifts of the Holy Spirit are meant to be part of the Church, until Jesus returns. 1 Cor 13:10

About these gifts, the Apostle Paul gave this counsel. They are given:

> for the common good 1 Cor 12:7
>
> as the Spirit determines 1 Cor 12:11
>
> each person has a gift 1 Cor 12: 1-11

each person's gift is important in the body 1 Cor 12:14

love* is vital to the gifts 1 Cor 13:1-3

We note that when Jesus did miracles, often he was moved with compassion for the person. The many different ways Jesus healed people, suggests that he was being prompted by the Holy Spirit in each situation. That is why there is no set method for the operation of the gifts.

Chapter 8

Our Attitude to the Holy Spirit

Valuing the Holy Spirit

I was in the shop of a client on business. The client was a Muslim. He was just about to talk to me when he was called out the back to take a phone call. As I waited, I noticed a letter on the counter from the leader of the local Mosque, urging all who read the letter to leave no stone unturned in their efforts to be totally devoted to their worship and practices. The letter told of many who were not getting to heaven because their efforts were less than total.

This letter made me think about the differences between our faiths, and also between our faith and Christian sects. Two differences between the Christian faith and Islam, is that in Islam there is no grace for lack of performance. The same is true of some Christian sects. One sect with which I am familiar insists on regular attendance at Church, which is marked down in a book.

In this sect, if for any reason people do not attend regularly, they are summoned before a judiciary panel to explain themselves and told that unless their performance improves, they are out and will be totally cut off from all fellowship. Ungrace prevails.

There are three distinct differences between religions like Islam, Christian sects, and Bible based Christianity.

- One is grace.

- The second difference is that we believe the Bible teaches we can have a relationship 'with', each member of the trinity. Our faith is not just 'us' and 'them' but 'we' - in relationship to each other.

- The third difference is the Holy Spirit.

There is no equivalent to the Holy Spirit in any other religion or sects. There are vague acknowledgments of the Holy Spirit in Christian sects but in my observation, there is no reality, and little attempt to teach what the Bible teaches about the Holy Spirit.

We Christians are so fortunate to have the Holy Spirit for he has been given for one, overall purpose. The following Scriptures indicate that one overall purpose. The Holy Spirit:

- teaches us John. 14:26

- reminds us of Jesus' teachings. John 14:26

- guides us into truth. John 16:13

- gives gifts to Christians for the building up of the Church. 1 Cor 12:7

- assist us to give an account of our faith. Luke 12:11

- testifies with our spirit that we are God's children Rom. 8:16

- helps us pray. Rom 8:27

The word that summarizes all these different actions of the Holy Spirit, is the word 'helper'. Some translations call the Holy Spirit 'the helper'. John 14.16 In Paul's second letter to

Timothy, he urged him to guard the deposit of sound   teaching,
"with the help of the Holy Spirit." 2 Tim 1.14 N.I.V

We Christians have the goal of finishing the race of faith. When we get to the finish line, it will be with the help of the Holy Spirit.

Much of the ground work in this chapter about valuing and appreciating the Holy Spirit has already been laid during the course of this book. In the first chapter, the point was made that the Holy Spirit is 'of God', sharing the same attributes and qualities as God the Father. Acts 5:3 &4.

In chapter three, readers were asked to think about the incredible intelligence of the Holy Spirit. An intelligence so great that he knows each of Earth's 6000 languages, and the earth's 1.8 billion Christians.

The Power of the Holy Spirit
Then there is the power of the Holy Spirit, a subject which has not been touched on in this book. In the book of Revelation, when the elders offered God worship, they offered God worship because

"You are worthy, our Lord and God,

> to receive glory and honor and power ..." Rev 4:11

In the Greek language, the word power is rendered - *Dynamis*. Rev 4:11. Jesus started his ministry

> "in the power (dynamis) of the Spirit." Luke 4:14

Jesus promised the disciples that they would receive (dynamis) 'power' when the Holy Spirit came upon them. Acts 1:8.

The Father, Son and Holy Spirit have immense dynamis - power.

Then there is the everywhereness (for lack of a better word), of the Holy Spirit. The prophet Joel said God would pour out his Spirit on 'all' people. Joel 2:28 That means of course, every people group between the Arctic and the Antarctic. People on every continent of the world.

David reiterated the idea that the Holy Spirit is everywhere, when he asked this question.

> "Where can I go from your Spirit,..."
> Psa 139:7.

It is inferred from this question that wherever we can go in the universe, we will find the Holy Spirit.

If we even 'begin' to grasp how amazing the Holy Spirit is, words like: respect, awe, amazement - are appropriate.

The Holy Spirit and God the Father are often viewed as being the same. The Holy Spirit is personal, immensely powerful, intelligent, and is everywhere in the universe.

Have you noticed the attitude of the other two members of the trinity, to the Holy Spirit? Jesus said to the disciples, "It is for your 'benefit' that I go away because if I do not, the Holy Spirit will not come."

We cannot tell if there was excitement and awe in the voice of Jesus when he spoke those words, but from the disciples point of view, it must have seemed incredible. Jesus was saying.

> Someone. Something, 'better' than me, is coming to replace me.

That same awesome respect for the Holy Spirit is implied in something else Jesus said. On one occasion he spoke about an unforgivable sin which has led to some believing that there are words they can say, or actions they can do (such as lying or stealing or adultery, or what-ever), and not be forgiven by God.

If Jesus words are read carefully, there is nothing we can say or do, and not be forgiven - with one exception. And that exception being:

> *"... anyone who says something against the Son of Man can be forgiven; but whoever says something against the Holy Spirit will not be forgiven – now or ever."* Matt 12:32 (GN)

There has been much debate in the Church about the unforgivable sin but that debate misses a significant point. Such was the respect for the Holy Spirit held by Jesus (and by implication – God the Father) that to openly speak against the Holy Spirit, is to say words that are unforgivable. Wow. Do you grasp what Jesus is saying? You or I can blaspheme God's name, but we will be forgiven if we sincerely ask God to forgive us. We can use Jesus' name in vain, and be forgiven, if we sincerely ask to be forgiven. However, that same grace does not apply to the Holy Spirit.

It is as if Jesus was saying. You might think the Holy Spirit is of lesser value, because you cannot see him – but the Father and I consider the Holy Spirit to be of such immense value and importance, that blaspheming the Holy Spirit, is the only unforgivable sin.

In Luke's' Gospel, Jesus indicated God's attitude to the Holy Spirit. He said, "If you then, though you are evil, know how to give good gifts to your children, how much more will your Father in heaven give the Holy Spirit to those who ask him!" (Luke 11:13 NIV)

In God's eyes then, the best gift he can give any person, is not a new car or an untroubled life, or great wealth and health. God's best gift to any person, is the Holy Spirit.

As I admitted at the beginning of this book, as a new Christian, I once thought of the Holy Spirit as merely like an electrical current who could be turned off and on. Or the Holy Spirit was like some divine mysterious vapor, that filled people. Eph 4:11

For all the reasons listed in this book so far , there has been a 'quantum change' in my attitude towards the Holy Spirit. It is now one of admiration and awe and appreciation.

What the Holy Spirit has done during nearly two millenniums of Church history, and will continue to do till Jesus returns, is similar to what was recorded of Jesus during his time on earth. About Jesus' time on earth, Paul wrote.

"Who, being in very nature God

did not consider equality with God

something to be grasped,

but made himself nothing, taking the very nature of a servant,

being made in human likeness.

And being found in appearance as a man,

he humbled himself and became obedient to death - even death on a cross!

Therefore God exalted him to the highest place

and gave him a name that is above every name,

that at the name of Jesus every knee should bow in

heaven and on earth,..."

Phil   2:8-10

(NIV)

These were the deserved accolades Jesus received after the completion of his mission on Earth. Many have probably not considered, that similar accolades will given to the Holy Spirit at the end of this age - and the completion of his mission to prepare the bride of Christ – the Church.

Those future accolades may read like this.

> The Holy Spirit, who is of very nature - God,

> *Who was with the Father in the creation of the heavens and earth,*

> and worked in tandem with Jesus to create the Church.

> *The Holy Spirit, who despite having limitless knowledge;*

> graciously and patiently waited to share that knowledge with any human beings, who would listen.

> *The Holy Spirit, who, despite having limitless power;*

> waited patiently to help any human, who was a disciple of Jesus.

> *The Holy Spirit, who despite being eternal, never once sought to glorify himself; but only sought to glorify the Father and the Son.*

> *Now honor is given to the Holy Spirit in heaven, because - for over two millenniums, the Holy Spirit interceded for individual Christians with the Father and sought to help them in numerous ways. He sought to build up the*

Church through giving guidance to disciples of Jesus. By giving them assurance and through giving them the fruits and gifts (of the Spirit).

Therefore.......

We do not know what words will follow the therefore .... but the Holy Spirit will be greatly honored for what he did for God's people in the Old Testament, during the ministry of Jesus, and in the Church since then.

Summary

As followers of Jesus, we need to recognize we are a temple of the Holy Spirit. 1 Cor 3:16. In other words, we humans are not merely mind, soul and body. We become a permanent temple or dwelling place, of the Holy Spirit.

Desiring the Holy Spirit
The Christian life has been compared to a long race, or a journey, or pilgrimage. It is a journey in which we can welcome the Holy Spirit to fill us daily and be our helper as we live life as a disciple of Jesus.

There are measures of the Holy Spirit in the life of a Christian.

- "Born of the Spirit."

- "Filled with the Spirit."

- "Anointed by the Spirit."

Jesus had a picture of his disciples as conduits of life-giving water, bringing life to dry arid soil. That picture of disciples as conduits of life-giving water is encapsulated in these words.

> "If anyone is thirsty, let him come to me and drink.".. Whoever believes in me, as the Scripture has said, streams of living water will flow from within him." By this he meant the Spirit, John 7:37

Following on, is a summary of the work of the Holy Spirit in the lives of individuals and the Church.

Holy Spirit - The creator

- Of the earth Gen 1.1

- Helps people create skillful artistic works Exod 31.3

- Creates new birth in an individuals life. John 3.6

Holy Spirit - The Educator

- Teaches us John 14.26

- Reminds us John 14.26

- Reveals God's truth 1 Cor 2.10

Holy Spirit - Who convicts, but does not condemn.

- My Spirit will not always strive with man Gen 6.4

Holy Spirit - The Evangelist

- Came upon Jesus, to preach the Gospel. Luke 4. 18-20

- Gave disciples many languages to convince foreign Jews. Acts 2.6&7

- Convicts people of sin. John 16.8

- Provides power to witness. Luke 4. 18 -20

Holy Spirit - Personal

- Assurance of Salvation Rom 8.16

- Assists in our prayer Rom 8..26

- Grows fruit in us Gal 5.22

Holy Spirit – works with, other members of trinity

- To bring glory to Jesus.

- Searches deep things of God 1Cor2.10

Holy Spirit - Guide

- Led Jesus John 4.1

- Leads us Rom 8.14

Holy Spirit and Church

- Gives gifts for the 'good' of the Church.
  1 Cor 12

World wide role

In the last days, God says,

I will pour out my Spirit on all people.

Your sons and daughters will prophecy,

your young men will see visions,

your old men will dream dreams.

even on my servants, both men and women,

I will pour out my Spirit in those days,

and they will prophecy.

I will show wonders in the heaven above

and signs on the earth below,

blood and fire and billows of smoke.

The sun will be turned to darkness and the moon to blood

before the coming of the great and

glorious day of the Lord.

And everyone who calls

on the name of the Lord will be saved.
Acts 2:17-21

But what can we say other than

"Come Holy Spirit"

About Philip Watson

I have grown up and live in New Zealand - Aotearoa (the Land of the Long White Cloud), currently residing in Auckland, our largest city with a population around 2 million people.

Around half of all New Zealanders live in Auckland. It is here that I can find the time to reflect on my faith and write.

It is the Bible and an intelligent and informed explanation of it's contents, that is the wind in the sails of the books I write. I am unashamedly evangelical or charismatic in my faith and my writings.

After finishing Theological College in New Zealand, I traveled to the Middle East to walk in the footsteps of Jesus, to glean a glimpse of the life he would have lived on this earth and soak in the ambiance of the world of Jesus and the glory of God's creations. This was for me a discovery of God and how important my Christian faith is for me, my family and my life.

I enjoy telling stories in my books, informing

and educating you, the reader, on our journeys. The richness of the history of the biblical lands and the truth of the Bible has moved me to reach out in Discipleship Books Ministry, an ordinary person helping other ordinary people find their faith in Jesus Christ, our savior.

These books I have put on Amazon are the culmination of 20 years of research, discovery and worship in the Christian Church. In many ways, these books map my journey as a Christian coming to grips with the meaning of being a true follower of Christ, and how to be the best disciple of Jesus I can be.

I pray that these insights I reveal in my books can create the same positive enlightenment in you as they have in me.